Power To Persist

Prayer Journal

Copyright 2016 Women Enlightened and Economically Empowered

Scripture taken from the New King James Version®. Copyright © 1982 by Thomas Nelson, Inc. Used by permission. All rights reserved.

Scripture taken from the HOLY BIBLE, NEW INTERNATIONAL VERSION®. Copyright © 1973, 1978, 1984 Biblica. Used by permission of Zondervan. All rights reserved. The "NIV" and "New International Version" trademarks are registered in the United States Patent and Trademark Office by Biblica. Use of either trademark requires the permission of Biblica.

Scripture quotations marked (NLT) are taken from the Holy Bible, New Living Translation, copyright © 1996, 2004, 2007 by Tyndale House Foundation. Used by permission of Tyndale House Publishers, Inc., Carol Stream, IL 60188. All rights reserved.

Scriptures from The Holy Bible, English Standard Version© (ESV©)
Copyright © 2001 by Crossway, a publishing ministry of Good News Publishers. All rights reserved. Used by permission. ESV Text Edition: 2007

Scriptures marked TLB are taken from the THE LIVING BIBLE (TLB): Scripture taken from THE LIVING BIBLE copyright© 1971. Used by permission of Tyndale House Publishers, Inc., Carol Stream, Illinois 60188. All rights reserved.

This journal is designed for the child of God who has a dream in their heart that they are committed to making a reality. We believe that God is the dream giver and He gives us visions and creative ideas for our future. As you pursue your dream, allow these scriptures to inspire you to keep pressing forward. No matter what the circumstance, put your faith and trust in God and let him give you the power to persist in pursuing your goals. Keep moving forward with thanksgiving in your heart and you will succeed! "Don't worry about anything; instead, pray about everything. Tell God what you need, and thank him for all he has done." Philippians 4:6, NLT
You can do it with God on your side!

Persistence

"Nothing in this world can take the place of persistence. Talent will not; nothing is more common than unsuccessful men with talent. Genius will not; unrewarded genius is almost a proverb. Education will not; the world is full of educated derelicts. Persistence and determination alone are omnipotent. The slogan Press On! has solved and always will solve the problems of the human race."

Calvin Coolidge
30th President of the United States
1923-1929

Deuteronomy 7:9

"Know therefore that the LORD your God is God; he is the faithful God, keeping his covenant of love to a thousand generations of those who love him and keep his commandments." NIV

Deuteronomy 28:13

"And the LORD will make you the head and not the tail; you shall be above only, and not beneath, if you heed the commandments of the LORD your God, which I command you today, and are careful to observe them." NKJV

Joshua 10:25a

"Joshua said to them, "Do not be afraid; do not be discouraged. Be strong and courageous." NIV

Psalm 3:3

"But thou, O LORD, art a shield for me; my glory, and the lifter up of mine head." KJV

Psalm 16:8

"I keep my eyes always on the LORD. With him at my right hand, I will not be shaken." NIV

Psalm 23:1

"The Lord is my Shepherd; I shall not want." KJV

Psalm 23:2-3

"He makes me lie down in green pastures. He leads me beside still waters. He restores my soul. He leads me in paths of righteousness for his name's sake." ESV

Psalm 23:4

"Even though I walk through the valley of the shadow of death, I will fear no evil, for you are with me; your rod and your staff, they comfort me." ESV

Psalm 23:5

"You prepare a table before me in the presence of my enemies; you anoint my head with oil; my cup overflows."
ESV

Psalm 23:6

*"Surely goodness and mercy shall follow me
all the days of my life, and I shall dwell in the house of
the L<small>ORD</small> forever."* ESV

Psalm 27:1

"The LORD is my light and my salvation; whom shall I fear? The LORD is the strength of my life; of whom shall I be afraid?" KJV

Psalm 27:14

"Wait on the LORD: be of good courage, and he shall strengthen thine heart: wait, I say, on the LORD." KJV

Psalm 31:3

"Since you are my rock and my fortress, for the sake of your name lead and guide me." NIV

Psalm 32:8

"The LORD says, "I will guide you along the best pathway for your life. I will advise you and watch over you." NLT

Psalm 34:8

"Taste and see that the LORD is good; blessed is the one who takes refuge in him." NIV

Psalm 34:19

"The righteous person may have many troubles, but the LORD delivers him from them all;" NIV

Psalm 34:22

"The LORD redeems the soul of His servants,
And none of those who trust in Him shall be condemned."
NKJV

Psalm 34:19

"The good man does not escape all troubles—he has them too. But the Lord helps him in each and every one." TLB

Psalm 37:4

"Be delighted with the Lord. Then he will give you all your heart's desires." TLB

Psalm 37:39
*"The LORD rescues the godly;
he is their fortress in times of trouble."* NLT

Psalm 42:5

"Why, my soul, are you downcast? Why so disturbed within me? Put your hope in God, for I will yet praise him, my Savior and my God." NIV

Psalm 46:1-3

"God is our refuge and strength, an ever-present help in trouble. Therefore, we will not fear, though the earth give way and the mountains fall into the heart of the sea, though its waters roar and foam and the mountains quake with their surging." NIV

Psalm 55:22

"Cast your cares on the LORD and he will sustain you; he will never let the righteous be shaken." NIV

Psalm 62:6

"He only is my rock and my salvation: he is my defence; I shall not be moved." KJV

Psalm 90:17

"And may the Lord our God show us his approval and make our efforts successful. Yes, make our efforts successful!"

NLT

Psalm 103:2

"Let all that I am praise the L<small>ORD</small>; may I never forget the good things he does for me." NLT

Psalm 118:14

"The LORD is my strength and my defense; he has become my salvation." NIV

Psalm 119:50

"My comfort in my suffering is this: Your promise preserves my life." NIV

Psalm 119:105

"Thy word is a lamp for my feet, a light unto my path." KJV

Psalm 119:114

*"You are my hiding place and my shield;
I hope in Your word."* NKJV

Psalm 120:1

*"In my distress I cried to the LORD,
And He heard me."* NKJV

Psalm 121:1-2

"I look up to the mountains— does my help come from there? My help comes from the L<small>ORD</small>, who made heaven and earth!" NLT

Psalm 121:7

*"He LORD will keep you from all evil;
he will keep your life."* ESV

Psalm 127:8

"He LORD will keep
your going out and your coming in
from this time forth and forevermore." ESV

Psalm 138:3

*"In the day when I cried out, You answered me,
And made me bold with strength in my soul."* NKJV

Psalm 145:18-19

"The LORD is near to all who call upon Him, to all who call upon Him in truth. He will fulfill the desire of those who fear Him; He also will hear their cry and save them." NKJV

Proverbs 2:7

"He stores up sound wisdom for the upright; He is a shield to those who walk uprightly;" NKJV

Proverbs 3:5-6

"Trust in the LORD with all your heart and lean not on your own understanding; in all your ways submit to him, and he will make your paths straight." NIV

Proverbs 10:22

*"The blessing of the LORD makes one rich,
And He adds no sorrow with it."* NKJV

Proverbs 16:3

*"Commit your actions to the LORD,
and your plans will succeed."* NLT

Isaiah 26:3

"You will keep in perfect peace all who trust in you, all whose thoughts are fixed on you!" NLT

Isaiah 40:31

*"But those who wait on the L*ORD *shall renew their strength; they shall mount up with wings like eagles, they shall run and not be weary, they shall walk and not faint."* NKJV

Isaiah 41:10

"Don't be afraid, for I am with you. Don't be discouraged, for I am your God. I will strengthen you and help you. I will hold you up with my victorious right hand." NLT

Isaiah 41:13

"For I am the LORD your God who takes hold of your right hand and says to you, Do not fear; I will help you." NIV

Isaiah 43:1

*"But now, thus says the LORD, who created you,
O Jacob, and He who formed you, O Israel:
"Fear not, for I have redeemed you; I have called you by
your name; you are Mine."* NKJV

Isaiah 43:2

"When you pass through the waters, I will be with you; and through the rivers, they shall not overflow you. When you walk through the fire, you shall not be burned, nor shall the flame scorch you." NKJV

Isaiah 54:17

"No weapon formed against you shall prosper, and every tongue which rises against you in judgment you shall condemn. This is the heritage of the servants of the LORD, and their righteousness is from Me," says the Lord." NKJV

Isaiah 58:11

"And the Lord will guide you continually, and satisfy you with all good things, and keep you healthy too; and you will be like a well-watered garden, like an ever-flowing spring." TLB

Lamentations 3:25
"The Lord is wonderfully good to those who wait for him, to those who seek for him." TLB

Lamentations 3:58

*"O Lord, you are my lawyer! Plead my case!
For you have redeemed my life."* TLB

Jeremiah 29:11

"For I know the plans I have for you," declares the LORD, "plans to prosper you and not to harm you, plans to give you hope and a future." NIV

Jeremiah 32:41

"I will rejoice in doing them good, and I will plant them in this land in faithfulness, with all my heart and all my soul." ESV

Nahum 1:7

"The LORD is good,
a stronghold in the day of trouble;
he knows those who take refuge in him." ESV

Zephaniah 3:17

"The LORD your God is with you, the Mighty Warrior who saves. He will take great delight in you; in his love he will no longer rebuke you, but will rejoice over you with singing." NIV

Matthew 6:25-26

"Therefore I tell you, do not worry about your life, what you will eat or drink; or about your body, what you will wear. Is not life more than food, and the body more than clothes? Look at the birds of the air; they do not sow or reap or store away in barns, and yet your heavenly Father feeds them. Are you not much more valuable than they?"

NIV

Matthew 7:7-8

"Ask and it will be given to you; seek and you will find; knock and the door will be opened to you. ⁸ For everyone who asks receives; the one who seeks finds; and to the one who knocks, the door will be opened." NKJV

Matthew 11:28

"Come to me, all who labor and are heavy laden, and I will give you rest." ESV

Mark 11:24

"Therefore I tell you, whatever you ask in prayer, believe that you have received it, and it will be yours." ESV

Matthew 17:20

"Because of your little faith," Jesus told them. "For if you had faith even as small as a tiny mustard seed, you could say to this mountain, 'Move!' and it would go far away. Nothing would be impossible. TLB

Matthew 19:26

"But Jesus beheld them, and said unto them, with men this is impossible; but with God all things are possible." KJV

Matthew 21:21

"Jesus replied, "Truly I tell you, if you have faith and do not doubt, not only can you do what was done to the fig tree, but also you can say to this mountain, 'Go, throw yourself into the sea,' and it will be done." NIV

Luke 10:19

"I have given you authority to trample on snakes and scorpions and to overcome all the power of the enemy; nothing will harm you." NIV

Luke 11:9-10

"And so I tell you, keep on asking, and you will receive what you ask for. Keep on seeking, and you will find. Keep on knocking, and the door will be opened to you. [10] For everyone who asks, receives. Everyone who seeks, finds. And to everyone who knocks, the door will be opened." NLT

John 14:27

"I am leaving you with a gift—peace of mind and heart! And the peace I give isn't fragile like the peace the world gives. So don't be troubled or afraid." TLB

John 15:4

"Remain in me, and I will remain in you. For a branch cannot produce fruit if it is severed from the vine, and you cannot be fruitful unless you remain in me." NLT

Romans 8:28

"And we know that in all things God works for the good of those who love him who have been called according to his purpose." NIV

Romans 8:31

"What then shall we say to these things? If God is for us, who can be against us?" ESV

Romans 8:37

"Yet in all these things we are more than conquerors through Him who loved us." NKJV

Romans 15:13

"Now may the God of hope fill you with all joy and peace in believing, that you may abound in hope by the power of the Holy Spirit." NKJV

1 Corinthians 2:5

"That your faith should not be in the wisdom of men but in the power of God." NKJV

1 Corinthians 2:9

"But as it is written: "Eye has not seen, nor ear heard, nor have entered into the heart of man the things which God has prepared for those who love Him." NKJV

1 Corinthians 10:13

"But remember this—the wrong desires that come into your life aren't anything new and different. Many others have faced the same problems before you. And no temptation is irresistible. You can trust God to keep the temptation from becoming so strong that you can't stand up against it, for he has promised this and will do what he says. He will show you how to escape temptation's power so that you can bear up patiently against it." TLB

1 Corinthians 15:57

"How we thank God for all of this! It is he who makes us victorious through Jesus Christ our Lord!" TLB

1 Corinthians 16:13

"Be on your guard; stand firm in the faith; be courageous; be strong." NIV

2 Corinthians 1:20

"For all of God's promises have been fulfilled in Christ with a resounding "Yes!" And through Christ, our "Amen" (which means "Yes") ascends to God for his glory." NLT

2 Corinthians 2:14

"Now thanks be to God who always leads us in triumph in Christ, and through us diffuses the fragrance of His knowledge in every place." NKJV

2 Corinthians 4:8-9

"We are pressed on every side by troubles, but not crushed and broken. We are perplexed because we don't know why things happen as they do, but we don't give up and quit. We are hunted down, but God never abandons us. We get knocked down, but we get up again and keep going." TLB

2 Corinthians 4:16

"That is why we never give up. Though our bodies are dying, our inner strength in the Lord is growing every day." TLB

2 Corinthians 5:7

"For we live by faith, not by sight." NIV

Ephesians 2:10

"For we are God's masterpiece. He has created us anew in Christ Jesus, so we can do the good things he planned for us long ago." NLT

Ephesians 3:16

"That He would grant you, according to the riches of His glory, to be strengthened with might through His Spirit in the inner man." NKJV

Ephesians 3:20-21

"Now to him who is able to do immeasurably more than all we ask or imagine, according to his power that is at work within us, to him be glory in the church and in Christ Jesus throughout all generations, for ever and ever! Amen." NIV

Ephesians 6:10-11

"A final word: Be strong in the Lord and in his mighty power. ⁱⁱ Put on all of God's armor so that you will be able to stand firm against all strategies of the devil." NLT

Philippians 4:6-7

"Don't worry about anything; instead, pray about everything. Tell God what you need, and thank him for all he has done. Then you will experience God's peace, which exceeds anything we can understand. His peace will guard your hearts and minds as you live in Christ Jesus." NLT

Philippians 4:8

"Finally, brethren, whatsoever things are true, whatsoever things are honest, whatsoever things are just, whatsoever things are pure, whatsoever things are lovely, whatsoever things are of good report; if there be any virtue, and if there be any praise, think on these things." KJV

Philippians 4:13

"I can do all things through Christ who strengthens me."
KJV

Philippians 4:19

"But my God shall supply all your need according to his riches in glory by Christ Jesus." KJV

Colossians 3:15

"And let the peace that comes from Christ rule in your hearts. For as members of one body you are called to live in peace. And always be thankful." NLT

2 Thessalonians 3:3

"But the Lord is faithful, and he will strengthen and protect you from the evil one." NIV

2 Timothy 1:7

"For God hath not given us the spirit of fear; but of power, and of love, and of a sound mind." KJV

2 Timothy 4:18

"And the Lord will deliver me from every evil work and preserve me for His heavenly kingdom. To Him be glory forever and ever. Amen!" NKJV

Hebrews 11:1

"Now faith is the substance of things hoped for, the evidence of things not seen." NKJV

Hebrews 2:18

"For in that He Himself has suffered, being tempted, He is able to aid those who are tempted." NKJV

James 1:2-4

"Consider it pure joy, my brothers and sisters, whenever you face trials of many kinds, because you know that the testing of your faith produces perseverance. Let perseverance finish its work so that you may be mature and complete, not lacking anything." NIV

James 1:6

"But when you ask, you must believe and not doubt, because the one who doubts is like a wave of the sea, blown and tossed by the wind." NIV

James 1:12

"God blesses those who patiently endure testing and temptation. Afterward they will receive the crown of life that God has promised to those who love him." NLT

1 Peter 5:7

"Let him have all your worries and cares, for he is always thinking about you and watching everything that concerns you." TLB

1 John 4:4

"Dear young friends, you belong to God and have already won your fight with those who are against Christ because there is someone in your hearts who is stronger than any evil teacher in this wicked world." TLB

1 John 4:18

"Such love has no fear, because perfect love expels all fear. If we are afraid, it is for fear of punishment, and this shows that we have not fully experienced his perfect love." NLT

1 John 5:4

"For everyone who has been born of God overcomes the world. And this is the victory that has overcome the world—our faith." ESV

1 John 5:14

"And we are confident that he hears us whenever we ask for anything that pleases him." NLT

1 John 5:15

"And if we know that he hears us in whatever we ask, we know that we have the requests that we have asked of him."

ESV

www.ingramcontent.com/pod-product-compliance
Lightning Source LLC
Chambersburg PA
CBHW031546040426
42452CB00006B/209